ISBN 9798355159269

Publisher: Beth Gross

Editing Services: Karla Heldenbrand

Cover Art: Neri Hurtado

DEDICATION

I would like to dedicate this book to the following.

First, to my loving and caring wife, Nancy, of 59 years of marriage. I love you so much.

Secondly, to our five loving and caring children, Beth, Phil, Julie, Kristen, and Amy. I love you so much.

Finally, to the Good Shepherd, the most loving and the most caring Shepherd and Savior. I commit to you all my love.

Table of Contents

Introduction

While living in Iran in 1972, I took a break one morning from translating the Old Testament books of Ruth and Esther. The rural culture of Iran and the ancient culture of Israel had striking similarities, and I was looking for some of them on that early morning trip to the nearby town. I was not prepared for what I experienced just outside that mud-walled village of Faraman.

Just as I was arriving the crude wooden doors of those mud walls flew open, and young 10- to 12-year-old shepherd boys dashed out with small flocks of 15-20 sheep dribbling out behind each one. The boys quickly began to chase each other, play tag, and throw small stones at each other. Then the sheep began to gather themselves together into one large flock. Without any human direction they began to drift down the slope from the village to a small stream. Again, without any direction, each began to drink deeply of the relatively slow-moving water. When all were well filled, still without any human direction, they ascended the slight slope on their own and waited silently.

Now another surprise for me. The boys stopped their playing and without any instructions took self-selected stations encircling the mixed flock. Next, it seemed to me, a near miracle unfolded. Suddenly all sorts of vocal sounds with no intelligible words, began to roll off the tongues and out of the throats of the young male shepherds. "Breeep," "glurlop," "stigup," etc. Miracle two exploded before my eyes! All the sheep became riveted, noses in the air, ears flopping on the side of each sheep head. The large flock disintegrated into little flocks of 15-20 woolen animals intently following only one sound. The boys moved away from the hub location of the big flock like spokes in a bicycle wheel, each continuing to make his distinct sound, with a small flock magnetized to its own young shepherd.

Amid this almost unbelievable drama, I whispered, barely audible, "My sheep hear my voice, and they follow me!"

Decades later, I arrived in India to train young pastors for the ministry. After serving as a missionary in Iran and the Philippines, we had settled in Indiana. I accompanied some of the pastoral staff of our home church to visit and encourage a young Indian pastor the church was supporting. During those visits I got to know Doctor Joy George and preached several times in the chapel of the seminary he directed in India.

Doctor Joy M. George, then president of ETS (Evangelical Theological Seminary) near Hosur, India, invited my wife, Nancy, and me to join the teaching faculty in India. We were thrilled at the invitation and quickly accepted his offer. However, when he began to explain what courses I would be teaching, I gently balked. He was appointing me to teach in the pastoral department. My two main courses would be pastoral ministry and homiletics. The homiletics assignment I understood. I had several years of pastoral experience in Missouri and Indiana. I also had cross cultural experience as a missionary and Bible translator which would be useful to me in developing my pastoral ministry course for India. But it was the training of young pastors for ministry in Indian culture and the surrounding cultures of India that gave me pause.

I argued, "Doctor George, you should recruit an alumnus of the seminary with a number of years of pastoral experience in Indian cultures to train young Indian pastors, not a foreigner who has never pastored an Indian culture church." But he insisted he knew what he was doing. I also learned quickly that no one challenges the president.

Back home in the U.S., I began preparation for teaching in India. I spent time praying and mulling over the pastoral ministry course. Then it began to come together. The heart of pastoring in any culture is shepherding the flock, the sheep. That thought triggered a memory of my experience in Iran. I had witnessed a drama that I had used in sermons for decades. Over 30 years later, this event would become the foundational lesson for young pastoral students in India. I would hold a young woolly lamb in my arms at the beginning of each class session. I would teach these pastors-in-the-making how to shepherd their sheep-congregations.

As the pieces of the course-structure began to form in my head I knew instinctively I had to secure permission from Doctor Joy to show up in class with a lamb. I formed a request that upon arriving in India, I would buy a lamb and bring him daily to the classroom and explain the shepherd-sheep roles in pastoring God's sheep-people. I would teach my students how to trust Jesus, the Good Shepherd.

Doctor Joy graciously granted permission for my request. In January 2008, having received my Doctor of Ministry degree in cultural anthropology in December from Grace Theological Seminary in Winona Lake, IN, we headed for India.

George Ragu, then the ETS Registrar, purchased the lamb from a local shepherd whom I never met. I paid 1,200 rupees for him (about $33.00 U.S.). The shepherd first brought a full-grown sheep, but I wanted a lamb.

He was a 3-month-old weaned male, just what I wanted. Out of all of the sheep I could have purchased, I bought him. I had enough money, but I would have sacrificed or would have made arrangements to get just the lamb I wanted.

I named him Cevesh (pronounced Ca-vesh, rhymes with fresh) which is the Hebrew word for lamb.

When I got him about 2 p.m., he already had the rope on his neck that I had purchased for him. Nancy and I took him for his first stroll around the campus to become familiar with his new home. I had checked out the campus. I knew where the best pastures were.

His first "leading" experience went well. He generally followed behind or along beside obediently. Sometimes he tugged at the end of the rope but was easily corrected. This would not always to be the case, as I was to learn later.

I immediately saw potential in him. He was healthy, alert, and responsive. This was going to be a good match.

I tied him outside my first-floor study window after our tour of the campus. He was a hit with the school kids. Later in the day I took Cevesh to meet and stay with his new keeper, the cook at ETS. As I left him, I explained, "Cevesh, I plan to spend one hour with you every morning for this whole semester, from 6:30 a.m. to 7:30 a.m."

The first morning I went to get Cevesh, I was deeply moved. He was standing tied up, looking my way, as though he was expecting me to come for him. How could he know that? This was our first day. He had had no experience prior to this morning. As soon as I saw him looking my way, I began to call him, "Brrrreeep," my special call to him. He was attentive when he heard that sound.

He seemed eager to go with me. He followed well, sometimes behind, sometimes alongside. But he was not always to be that compliant to being led. When we got to the beginning of the good pasture, he pulled a little trick that I learned later he would pull quite often. When his desire and my plan differed, he dropped down on his two front knees and refused to go any further.

Though I had grown up on a farm and had experience with cattle and hogs, we had never had a sheep hoof on the property. As a new shepherd, I was surprised at this sudden show of self-will.

I had a choice. I knew the best pasture was further down the lane. I could drag or carry him; I was stronger and knew best. However, my ultimate goal was for Cevesh to trust and obey me. He was in good pasture now. I decided to let him graze there. I took the bucket I had brought to sit on and the book I had brought to read, and I began reading to him. Of course, I knew he did not understand one word I was reading, but my purpose was for him to get to know the sound of my voice.

He immediately began to forage away the good pasture, not paying any attention to me but obviously hearing my voice as I read. I watched him as he chose some plants and rejected others. He definitely had favorites.

After 15-20 minutes, his initial appetite satisfied, he did something that was a complete surprise to me. Without me calling or inviting him, he stopped eating and voluntarily came over to me, put his head up on my knee, and just stood there.

I could hardly believe it! He sought me! It was just what I wanted, but I never could have forced him to do this. For several minutes he stayed there, and I scratched his head, petted him, and talked very tenderly to him. I told him how great friends we would become as time went by.

Getting sheep to trust the shepherd is a journey. It is a spiritual journey, a long and sometimes difficult journey. It has its ups and downs, its varying speeds, and its progress and stumbling.

If you commit with me to the journey, I will explain the lessons that I and my lamb, Cevesh, taught each other. It is worth all the effort necessary to learn to trust the shepherd.

Chapter 1

Trusting the Shepherd in the Transfer of Ownership

The first step in this long but exciting journey is how to be born into the Shepherd's family, metaphorically speaking, becoming his sheep. In the physical world sheep get new owners by being bought. In the spiritual realm the process is also, in one facet, similar. Christ bought us by the purchase of his own blood.

But it should be noted that the dissimilarity is huge. In the physical realm the amount of money paid out will result in the number of sheep purchased. But in the spiritual realm one price bought all the sheep. That same full price would have been necessary for just one sheep. The writer of the Book of Revelation explains:

> And they sang a new song, saying,
> " Worthy are you to take the scroll
> and to open its seals,

for you were slain, and by your blood you ransomed people for God from every tribe and language and people and nation, and you have made them a kingdom and priests to our God, and they shall reign on the earth." (Revelation 5:9)

There is a huge distinction in the process of purchasing. In the physical realm the sheep have no say in the matter of a new ownership. However, in the spiritual realm the sheep do have say in the transition of ownership. The spiritual sheep *must* agree to the transition. Each individual people-sheep must want and desire a new owner-shepherd. The apostle John in Revelation 3:20 expresses that desire in these terms, "Behold, I stand at the door and knock. If anyone hears my voice and opens the door, I will come in to him and eat with him, and he with me." That desire is further expressed in terms of putting one's faith in the new shepherd and his blood-price (Hebrews 9:11, Romans 1:16, 3:25, 4:5, 5:2, etc.).

Only when sheep have changed shepherd-ownership will he hear the shepherd's voice and follow him (John 10:27).

Imagine that Cevesh began to express his new life this way: "I know you are my new owner and master and that my life will be better now than it was before, but I don't understand very much about what this new life is all about.

"When you bought me, it cost me my original family. I'm only three months old, and I've really missed my mommy. I am very tempted to want to go back to my original family and live the way I used to live."

The shepherd (me) responded: "When I first bought you, I took you to *my* home to get you used to what is now *your* new home, to see some of the good pasture places, and to spend some time together to get to know each other a little bit. You laid in my lap for about 30 minutes and listened to me talking to you in soft tones. Of course, you didn't understand what it meant."

"Shepherd, I miss my family. But when I was with them, I was learning some things from them about the things they do. Do you think I need to be with some other sheep while I'm growing up? Could they teach me some 'sheep stuff' that I might not learn by myself?"

"Cevesh, you have a good point about needing to be with other sheep. You could probably learn some good sheep lessons on growing up and sheep maturity from some older sheep that would make good teachers for you. But right now, that is not possible, so you are going to have to trust me and learn from me. We'll see what the future holds for us. Trust me for now."

One of the young pastoral students made the following observation about Cevesh's transition from his old life to his new life. "Cevesh enjoyed his life with his family, he never thought that there would be life beyond what he had with his family. But a day came when he had to leave his loved ones and belong to someone else. He had no clues of what his tomorrow would be. The new shepherd bought him with a price from his old master so that he could train and equip him for a greater purpose. He was the chosen one among the flock of sheep, chosen not by his strength or ability but by the sheer mercy of the shepherd who purchased him. He had no contribution in the transaction; it was all done by the shepherd."

Chapter 2
Trusting the Shepherd as You Grow in
Understanding

To grow in trusting the Shepherd, one must learn how to understand the Bible. The Bible can be likened to a volume that combines all the primary readers from first to eighth grades into one book. It contains many kinds of literature and can be read and understood at different levels depending on the reader's level of education. As his level of education and experience increases, so would his ability to fathom the truth of scripture. Portions of the Bible above his reading level would be virtually not understood.

Beyond the secular education that would equip one to understand the Bible, there is another qualification that is much more relevant in understanding the truth of the written Word of God. I refer to the presence of the indwelling Spirit of God. He resides in each believer and not only empowers him to walk a godly life but is the main factor in understanding the written Word of God.

Let me unfold and apply this vital principle. The Holy Spirit is the Bible's author. Throughout its pages the Holy Spirit is acknowledged as the one who reveals the truth recorded in its pages, and the one who determines what events and conversations are recorded in the book. It is obvious to acknowledge that one of the most accurate ways to understand a written document is to be in conversation with its author.

The Holy Spirit works in our spirit, particularly our minds, and sheds light on statements in the text that otherwise would be meaningless to the reader. This aspect of his indwelling in our essence is important in this regard. His omniscience functions in relationship to our vocabulary, experiences, and the level of our spiritual growth. He shows and teaches us things that we can't fully understand on an academic level and applies scripture to our lives on a spiritual level.

Taking it a step further, the Holy Spirit is aware of the unique spiritual progress of each believer. Each believer-reader of the Bible has many facets of his being and skills of understanding that are distinct from any other believer-reader. For instance, two believers can sit side-by-side listening to an exposition and reading the same text of scripture, but their perception or understanding of the text may seem light years apart. The difference is discovered in the skill of the Holy Spirit opening the truth in that moment that centuries previously he had guided and recorded in the text of scripture.

Another principle is the level of Bible content education that a believer-reader brings to the exercise. This is particularly true of the knowledge of the Old Testament history and the depth of meaning of its revelation. Often a young child picks up this knowledge in Sunday School classes while growing up in church. Other times this knowledge is acquired under the skillful exposition of scripture by a pastor. It can even be acquired by one's own energetic dedication to self-study of the Bible.

An example maybe helpful. In reading the documents of the apostle Paul and the apostle Peter, one can sense a universe of difference in perception in the texts of these two writers. Though both were Jews, and both were converted in the same century, yet the Bible content knowledge of the apostle Paul from his training as a Pharisee is far beyond that of the basic synagogue training that the apostle Peter received.

The final principle is the desire to know the Word of God. The driving hunger, particularly of a new believer, is rewarded by the Holy Spirit in opening truths to his heart that the less eager reader will miss.

Now let's turn to my lamb's explanations. Cevesh says it like this, "Shepherd, I hear you reading every morning while I'm grazing, but I really don't understand a word you're saying. Do you realize you are way over my head? You may be saying good stuff, but I'm not getting it. Is that a problem for you?"

The shepherd responded, "Before I started reading my book aloud to you, I had a little conversation with you that went something like this, 'I know you will come to trust me more in the future. As we spend time together, you will learn to follow me better. Now I'm going to read to you. You probably won't understand what I'm reading, but you will get used to *hearing my voice,* and you will learn to recognize *my voice* when I speak.'"

Chapter 3

Trusting the Shepherd as You Learn New Truths and Skills

"Shepherd, have you noticed that I do have a will of my own, and that I don't always do exactly what you want me to do? I am not a "robot." I basically like to please you, but sometimes I really want to have my own way. But I have noticed that you patiently wait and finally change my way to your way. Ultimately your way is always better, but I don't always see it at first. You don't always explain it to me. And even if you did, I probably would not comprehend it because your ways are higher than my ways. "

Building on our last step, we are introduced to the world of learning new things. This experience will follow us the rest of our lives in one form or another.

Learning goes beyond awareness and even understanding. The heart of learning is absorption and application, being able to reproduce concepts and skills.

Learning also includes the new, fresh, or previously unknown. Truths that were not understood, not perceived. Often these new things catch us off guard. They may be uncomfortable, at times, even painful. The new tends to take us away from the old, easy, and comfortable. What we have learned to do in the past that has become effortless is being replaced with activities that require new, even difficult effort.

We tend to resist. We may complain and argue for things to remain the same as they presently are. The strong walls of this resistance is often drawn from the *history* of our experiences and the experiences of others, even famous practitioners of our actions. Note the leverage of our *history*. Our perspective is seldom of how the future could be changed for the better. We worship the past and strongly resist change in the future.

Maybe you can relate to Cevesh. As he is learning, he is also resistant to learning new things.

"Shepherd, I noticed that you changed the grazing place the other day. I like the change, but I was a little surprised the first day when we did not go back the same place, I have gone there for over five weeks. I really didn't know what you were doing. But I like the new place. Besides, I'm learning some things in this new place that I could never have learned in the old place.

"You have also begun to teach me to climb stairs. Already I have learned to go all the way from the ground to our classroom all by myself. Are you proud of me? I thought you would be. Really it was not hard for me to learn that. But you were so surprised that I learned it so quickly. I was created to climb because some of my natural pasture is in very difficult areas, and I must climb around rocks to get to my food. So, you should not have been surprised at all. Learning to climb stairs was easy for me."

"Cevesh, we have another area we need to discuss this morning. It involves the stairs. You learned how to climb them so quickly. But the problem is that you stop on the landings and look around and won't respond to my call. Sometimes I even must come up and get you started to go up or come down the stairs. We are going to have to practice until you can readily obey my voice when I call you up or down the stairs. That you have learned how to do stairs is not enough. You must get past resistance and learn obedience. OK? OK!

"You are learning many things these days, and I am very proud of you. Yes, you do surprise me at some of the things you have learned and can do. I don't think I really knew that you were a natural climber."

"Shepherd, you really surprised me on my one-month anniversary with you as my new owner. A bath, a scrub-down, is hardly what I was expecting. I see we really do live in two different worlds. Your ways are higher than mine. But a bath???? When you put me up on that one-meter-high washer block, I had no idea what the water and the soap and the brush were all about. In fact, I tried to jump off a couple of times, but you restrained me. After that I was willing to stand very still while you scrubbed my legs and the stains in my wool. But Shepherd, you are going to have to find a better cleaning agent because the stains are still there. I'm clean. But I'm still stained. Is there going to be another bath in the future???"

"Shepherd, you also have been teaching me to lie down. That is harder for me to learn from you. I already know how to lie down, but I don't always want to lie down when you want me to. I have not learned very well what your command is, and I have not learned to be obedient to your command on this action. But I am working on it. Soon I will probably be obedient every time you tell me to lie down."

"Cevesh, there is one area that you have a lot of work left to do. It is that matter of the little yellow blossoms that fall off the four trees between here and the kitchen. They probably are not bad for you, but if you eat all that you wanted to eat, you probably would get sick. But that is not my greatest concern. Here is the problem. On our way to and from the cafeteria and to the classroom and back, we do not have the time to eat all the fallen blossoms that you want. There is plenty for you to eat at both ends of our trip but not during the trip. You must learn to obey me and follow me. Eating the blossoms is not bad, but not obeying is bad. We have to "get past the yellow blossoms." Something tells me that is going to be a difficult thing for you to learn. It may take a long time, but I am committed to you learning to be able to walk through the fallen blossoms without stopping. Can you do this? I hope so.

"I noticed something very interesting this week about your eating habits. I'll call it selective eating. You not only demonstrated discernment in what you ate, but I also notice the great variety of what you ate. You are not like a goat that eats anything and everything in sight, but you do have great variety. I call that balanced eating. I like that. I, as your shepherd, will see to it that you have great variety in the pastures that I lead you to."

"Cevesh, you are a sheep. I am a man. As I am teaching you, I'm also committed to you and your well-being and future. But sometimes I am not as focused on you and your needs as I should or could be. You'll have to accept that and forgive me sometimes when I fail you. I want you to know that this is my first shepherding experience. Even though I have been one of God's sheep for many years and learned how to be a good sheep in His flock, this is my first experience in leading other sheep. Be patient with me as I will be with you. OK?

"I enjoy being with you, but I don't always understand what I experience with you. Sometimes after we are together, I talk to my wife about what you do and about how I'm feeling about it. It is good to have someone else to share what is going on between us. In fact, after I talk to her, sometimes things seem more understandable. You may not be able to understand that, but it is important to me."

The student Patir observed, "Cevesh is a sheep, and I came to know what really sheep need. How important it is to see a sheep as the shepherd did. It was a little difficult [to] see why it was necessary to obey or to listen to the shepherd. The sheep started to listen [and] came to recognize the shepherd's voice then started to accompany with the shepherd. He gave me a great lesson [of] being a sheep of God. We also sometimes disobey God or are unfaithful to God. We can be faithful to God [and] obey our shepherd or master. It encouraged me and gave me hope to know how much our shepherd cares."

Another student, Singh, shared these lessons he learned. "I learned many good lessons from Cevesh. He drew my attention [to] future ministry. I felt compassionate about the lost, those who are living in the darkness. One of the interesting things that I learned from Cevesh is meekness, he is very obedient and very fast to learn. Of course, Cevesh is an animal but compared to other animals I realize that God used sheep as an illustration to show the meekness and humbleness to the man."

My student Paubiaksang learned these deep insights. "From Cevesh, I have learned certain things as mentioned below. 1. Sheep know the voice of the shepherd and tend to follow the words coming out of the mouth of the shepherd. Likewise, believers should recognize the voice of our Shepherd (God) and follow his words. 2. Cevesh only follows the shepherd, he is reluctant to follow any other person. In other words, no other person except the shepherd can pull him wherever he wants him to go. Likewise, believers should follow God alone not the devil or anyone else. 3. Even when Cevesh rebels against the shepherd, the shepherd continues to care for him compassionately. In the same way, God takes care of us and loves us even when we are disobedient and rebellious. God loved us when we were sinners. 4. Cevesh did not initially know where the green pastures were, he was led there by the shepherd. Likewise, God leads us to the place where green pastures are available. He supplies spiritual food for us in the form of the Word of God."

Another student Mung felt some deep lessons. "Sheep are obedient and teachable. He is fast and learning things and aware of his surroundings. Therefore, from him I can learn about obedience, be teachable and be aware of the surroundings that can harm me. It really teaches me a lesson."

Student Thang learned multiple lessons. "Lessons learned from Cevesh: 1. I learned that sheep need a good, compassionate, and patient shepherd. Pastors should shepherd the flock with compassion and patience 2. Sheep can be disobedient and stubborn at times. The pastor should be understanding of the problems and struggles of the people. 3. Sheep sometimes need to be disciplined. The pastor should be courageous to tell the truth boldly when needed."

Again, Kia weighs in with some significant insights. "The shepherd bought Cevesh with the purpose, and he trained toward fulfilling that purpose. On the other hand, Cevesh did not realize his purpose and lived as he liked. He didn't know where he was going but the Shepherd knew exactly where he would lead. The shepherd's plan for Cevesh is all good and beneficial, but the lamb did not realize this but was always seeking to gratify his desires.

"Likewise, God knows every detail of my life and despite my desires and sinful ways he continues to lead me that I may reach the destination which God planned for. Everything he has really is good and has eternal value. Many times, I suppress the purpose of God in my life and live for the things of the world."

Now let's examine the insights of another student. "On his life journey, sometimes Cevesh fell into the pit, sometimes he plays in mud and gets it all over his body, yet he cannot get clean by himself. He needs someone to clean him from his dirt. Eventually, the shepherd is there to take care of him. The shepherd cleans Cevesh when he is need of cleansing and this is an ongoing process, sometimes he may need two times a day or even more. Regardless of his habits the Shepherd's love for him never changes.

"Cevesh has taught me that I cannot clean myself from my sin, I need to go to Jesus Christ for cleansing and forgiveness. As Cevesh needs cleansing again and again, I also need regular cleansing by the Lord from my daily sins, and he is always there with the same amount of love despite my wretched behavior."

Chapter 4

Trusting the Shepherd as He Carries You

Now it seems wise to attempt to explain the topic of "being carried." Referring to a sheep, the action is obvious. The shepherd decides for any number of reasons to pick up the lamb and carry it to the destination of his choice. The similarities to the Christian life may not seem so obvious, however there are parallel choices that the Good Shepherd makes.

First, danger lurks in places where we are unaware. The all-knowing Good Shepherd can sense danger either of the natural sort or of that planned by the enemy. Particularly when we are new to our faith, the ability to be aware of either kind of danger is not yet in our repertoire of skills. The Good Shepherd reaches down and lifts us up to safety in his skillful protecting arms. An example could be a young but undiscerning believer in a new workplace that is a stronghold of Satan.

Another reason we may be carried is our inability to keep up with the flock, that is, the planned program or timing of events for our lives. We are most likely unaware of these times of being carried which are precipitated by undeveloped skills which will be developed later in our pilgrimage. An example from a ministry setting might be an inexperienced worker in a fast-moving team.

The knowledgeable shepherd may also need to carry us over terrain through which we are stumbling. As gifted as sheep are in traveling rough terrain, there are always rocky cliffs and valleys that sheep, especially young lambs, are unable to safely traverse. For example, a disabling health experience of a person or their family member that totally disrupts their work and family life.

Rebellion is another reason for transporting a sheep. Rebellion may have many different drivers, and the shepherd has several options for dealing with it that apply to lambs and to us and our Good Shepherd. For instance, the shepherd could continue with his obedient flock and leave the rebellious lamb to his own ultimate destruction. Another response of our shepherd could be to drag the young willful lamb along the path. Depending on the method of dragging and the roughness of the surface, the sheep would suffer cuts and bruises. The experience would breed bad feelings in the sheep against his otherwise kind shepherd. Or the shepherd could stop with the lamb and wait for us to change our minds and become compliant to his plan.

Being carried builds our confidence in our shepherd's ability and in his gentleness. We are not usually aware of most "carrying" in the moment. Only later when we can look back on those rough places of our lives do we become aware that we were carried by our shepherd, the great one, the good one.

Cevesh began to catch on about being carried. "Shepherd, I have noticed that lately when I lay down along the way, you don't carry me as far as you used to carry me. You just carry me a short distance, set me down again, and I begin walking. In fact, I think you have stopped carrying me and just pick me up and set me on my feet when I lay down, and I start walking again."

Kia described it this way. "The beauty of all this drama is that the shepherd understands Cevesh's struggles and loves him even more when he failed. The shepherd is always there to help, to lift him up and carry him when he falls, encourage him when he is depressed, to cheer [him] up when he fights the battle. The Shepherd knows what the sheep has gone through and come what may, the shepherd will never, ever give up on him."

Chapter 5

Trusting the Shepherd by Choosing to Follow

Life with the shepherd is a lot like a conversation. Once we become his sheep, we learn his voice and naturally follow him. But there are times when that responsive following turns into "stops."

"Shepherd, did you notice my stops the other day. These are not the same as distractions. Stops are different. We are walking along, and I just stop. I'm not sure why I do that sometimes. I just don't like to be told what to do all the time. There are times when I want to make the decision and not just go along with what you want me to do."

"Cevesh, I untied you and you readily followed me, sometimes right beside me, because I was headed for the good pasture. When we got to the beginning of the grass, Cevesh, you stopped, dropped to your knees, and wouldn't go any farther. But this wasn't where the best grass was. It was further down the road. Now I had a choice. Either I could force you by dragging you or carrying you, or I could let you eat this grass. I let you have your own way for a short while. Then I made you follow me.

"Immediately after I decided you could stay there and not force you to go on further, you began to hungrily eat the grass. You seemed starved. I watched you carefully to see which plants you ate and which you rejected. You really do have favorites."

"Shepherd, I'm becoming very choosy in what I eat when I'm with you. I do have a wide appetite for different plants. But when I'm in the good grazing place with you I choose what I like best. Since I have been following you to the same place for several weeks now, I know what plants are there and just where the plants are that I like best. I don't have to hunt for them much. I can go right to the good stuff."

"Cevesh, I want to talk to you about Direction-Correction. When you graze you seem oblivious to where you are going. Sometimes you wander too far from me, and I must correct your direction. That is not new. What is new is how easily you are corrected. Sometimes I merely call you and you return. But usually, I must turn you around and point you in the right direction. But you are responding very well to my corrections. You are making good progress in Direction-Correction. Keep up the good work."

"Cevesh, I don't think I'll ever be able to tell you the pleasure and the joy I get when I see you learning and obeying me so willingly. Your maturing and obedience bring great joy to me. You may not ever be aware of my joy, but it's real, and it makes all the effort and all the waiting worthwhile. You are making progress, and I can see it. Keep up the good work."

Now some of the students want to share lessons they learned. I'll let Haming begin.
"This is what I've learned from Cevesh and why. Negative lessons: 1. He is stubborn. Sometimes he failed to listen to the shepherd's voice. 2. He trusts his own instincts which sometimes made him lack trust in the

shepherd's command. 3. He sometimes ended up in confusion when he chose not to listen to the chief Shepherd or the under shepherd. Most often it was due to want of food or grazing.

"Positive lessons: 1. He is a quick learner. The bond between the sheep and the shepherd as it is depending mostly on the part of the Shepherd, but then the sheep learns to differentiate the voices of the shepherds. 2. He can communicate fast to the voice of the Shepherd and follow the footsteps of the Shepherd without tying his rope on his neck. 3. He learned to trust in the shepherd and can take refuge in the shepherd which could be seen when he feels danger from other animals. He is very alert of his surroundings at the same time."

Another student Thang observed, "Sometimes Cevesh rebels and doesn't like to listen to what Dr. Dale said! So also, being a shepherd sometimes our church members may rebel and not want to listen to us. But we can keep calm and handled gently to win."

Student Kia contributes, "Cevesh most of the time would prefer to be his own master than submitting to the will of the shepherd. Cevesh taught me that I am not better than him. I confessed with my mouth that I love God but most of the time I resist him and would like him to agree to my terms and wishes. The funny thing is that I learned so much from Cevesh but even then, I find it very difficult to apply what I have learned in my life.

"Though, at times, Cevesh rebelled against the shepherd's will, but the Shepherd's decision is the final and will not be changed for any reason.

"Many times, Cevesh grieved the shepherd. Not only that, but he also shamed his shepherd in front of others because of his rebellious acts. I also have grieved the Lord many times."

Chapter 6

Trusting the Shepherd to Untangle My Problems

"Shepherd, I figured out something today that I haven't known before. Sometimes I get all tangled up in the vines where I am grazing, and sometimes I get all tangled up in my rope. But I have learned something very important. I cannot get myself untangled from either the vines or the rope by myself. I have also learned that only you know how to get me untangled and back to my free self-grazing again. Thank you, Shepherd, for seeing my problem and coming to help me out every time I get all tangled up."

Cevesh's conversations about entanglements are enlightening as we consider our personal problems. Sometimes life is like hair. It gets all tangled up! There are two types of "tangles." One type of tangle happens virtually every day because we sleep the whole night without protection around our hair. The other type of tangle is more serious and is impossible to untangle without radical outside help.

In life, daily tangles are the daily problems and challenges of living in a fallen world. They are repetitive. They often appear in the same place at the same time for the same reasons. However, it doesn't make that tangle any less of a problem. They seem like minor challenges because we have faced them before, and we have worked through them many times. Consequently, we can usually untangle the mess ourselves.

Observers have a repetitive response to our daily dilemmas. It goes something like this, "You broke it; you fix it." "You spilled it; you wipe it up." "You lost it; you find it." However, the verdict of judges who observe our lives may not have all the facts. To be sure, many of our messes are of our making. But not always. Because we are so deeply involved with our entanglements, it would appear that we have caused them, and the repetition of the problem might lend credence to that conclusion.

But we must remember that Satan is our great enemy who walks about seeking whom he may devour. Since we have dealt with him in the past on this issue, we are equipped to claim the blood of Christ, defeat our enemy, and untangle ourselves.

Repeated tangles can lead to deep discouragement. One thing that helps in coping with discouragement is to remind ourselves that the tangle can be undone. We have worked ourselves out of that tangle previously, even if it had happened many times before.

Now, let's turn to the more serious tangles. These entanglements usually include elements that we may have not dealt with previously. Metaphorically speaking, there may be hairclips, twigs, or nothing more than exceedingly knotted hair in this swirled tangle. Whatever the particulars of the tangle are, they are beyond the scope of our comb, brush, and mirror. At this point, we must call in the troops! But as impossible as this scene may appear, it is no challenge for the Good Shepherd.

The strategy of our commander may not appear effective. As with Joshua, his instruction to repeatedly circle the enemy and wait for his timing may raise doubts in our minds as we wait for a defeat and an undoing of the entanglement. But if his instructions are patiently followed, the walls will fall!

The repetitiveness of our life entanglements often sows doubt in our minds as to whether we really are on the right track and have the right relationship to our leader-shepherd. Analyzing doubts can be a major step in causing them to dissolve completely. Remember, we live in a fallen world that remains in its fallen condition our entire lifetime. Further, just because we had victory over the tangles of the past does not discourage Satan from constantly attempting to drag us back into his problem-land.

How to we prevent tangles? First of all, avoid the situations where tangles most likely have appeared. At first, we may not have associated tangles with these relationships, but as time goes on, we grow in wisdom and can see them coming down the road of life. Avoidance can become one of the wisest concepts in our spiritual lives.

Another strategy is what I call "strong resistance." In some cases, simply avoiding places and situations isn't enough. There may be continuous and persistent pressure involved in the tangle. Thus, extra persistence to resist is necessary.

We must remember that victory is sure. It has been in the past; it will be presently and even in the future should it appear again. The certainty of victory cannot be over emphasized. No matter how low or deep the discouragement may be, this ray of light at the end of the tunnel is certainly a powerful encouragement to press on out of the entanglement.

The last perspective I want to discuss on untangling our lives from problems is what results from our victories over our struggles. Occasionally, we grow by observing others or reading about entanglements, but most of life's growth, physical or spiritual, comes from experiencing difficulties. Yes, the "School of Hard Knocks." One of the obvious reasons that this is so true in life is that we develop through stages of growth. An infant cannot understand let alone experience many of the things that a teenager or an adult must go through while maturing. Likewise, growth-tangles are necessary in spiritual development.

Our victory over life-tangles also equips us to help others going through similar problems. We may observe a fellow believer struggling with an entanglement that he or she seems to be exhibiting no skills to win a victory. Often if we come alongside and offer help, we are welcomed with open arms. The confession that "I have been there, done that," can bring hope to the heart of the entangled.

Our victories become "models" for others who may not currently be struggling with our tangle but in wisdom will note how we won the victory and will file it back in their memory for future reference. "Modeling" impacts unbelievers as well as believers.

Chapter 7

Trusting the Shepherd in Freedom of Maturity

Next, there is the matter of that "rope." Cevesh continues. "I'm not sure I like the basic idea that it suggests, at least, to my way of thinking. Don't you trust me? It's not that I'm trying to run away from you. Have I ever tried to leave you yet? Aren't you my shepherd and aren't I your sheep? So? What's with the rope? It's always in my way. I'm always getting tangled up in it and then you must come untangle me. Wouldn't it save you a lot of time and hassle if we didn't have this restraining rope? No rope, OK?

In the early weeks when I was bringing my lamb, Cevesh, to class there was a strong focus on the use of the rope to lead and correct the lamb's activities. The young pastoral students were fascinated by the rope. They gradually grew in their insight of the need of the rope, of the growing trust and obedience between shepherd and sheep, and the implications of the paradigm for the pastor and congregation.

I will unfold insights on the use and meaning of the rope in the sheep's experience and in ours. Note the length of the rope. The shepherd determines the length of the rope based on his sovereign desire of the distance he is willing to admit between himself and his sheep. The sheep never seems to be aware of this predetermined decision of the rope's length, although all the activities between the shepherd and his sheep are measured by the rope. Some of the activities seem to be totally unaffected by the presence of the rope, however, other activities are limited and adjusted by its length.

Basically, the rope works against the resistance of the sheep. Either the woolly one resists the direction the shepherd desires to go, or the shepherd resists the direction the sheep desires to go. The rope guarantees that in each case the distance between the shepherd and his sheep will remain constant. While roped to the shepherd, the sheep never gets lost or strays. Though the sheep is often displeased with the effect of the rope, the sovereign condition of closeness that the rope creates between the shepherd and the sheep is undeniably good.

Another aspect of the rope is that it keeps the shepherd and sheep close to one another. The opposite of this concept is "out of sight, out of mind." Being close to one another creates the awareness of one's presence and needs. But while separated there is a lack of growth in the relationship. Togetherness builds the atmosphere of working together and learning to adjust to each other. All these parallel truths of our spiritual relationship to Christ, by the way, also applies to the marriage relationship.

The rope also corrects the will, direction, and activities of the sheep. It is particularly important to note that only the shepherd has the sovereignty of "rope-correction." At no time in the relationship does the sheep have the rope around the shepherd's neck. Obviously, the omniscient Shepherd never needs correction, particularly from his own sheep. However, often the created sheep needs "shepherdly" correction.

The final aspect of the rope is the times when the rope is off or on. It is obvious that when the shepherd and his young sheep are traveling from one location to another, the rope is a necessity. Even after the destination has been reached, the presence of the rope is still a necessity. However, when the sheep has been returned to his pen, the rope is no longer necessary and will be released from the sheep's neck. Though this metaphorical use of the rope is easy to understand, we sheep may not be able to discern our "pen-experience." Our "home-pen" experience could refer to our after-work hours in the evenings or our days off. It is those relaxed periods in our lives when the pressure is off, the demanding activities are not required, and we are not in the limelight.

My conversations with Cevesh about his rope over the months have a lot of metaphorical application of our experience with the Good Shepherd. Listen carefully to our interchange.

"Shepherd, the other day was the first day you took my rope off when we got to the grazing place. It felt so good not to have that rope dragging through the grass and weeds while I grazed. I stayed very close to you most of the time. One time I got too far away from where you were sitting. When you called me, I turned completely around and came all the way back to you. You looked so pleased when I did that. You even looked very surprised. Were you really surprised that I know your voice and come to you when you call me?"

"Cevesh, you are learning and developing well for just being 3 months old. This week I have been taking your rope off when we get about 10 meters away from the good grazing place. Every day you have come all the rest of the way by yourself and began grazing right beside me. When we return to the shed, I have been untying your rope about 50 meters away and you have followed me very well all the way back. I will continue to lengthen that distance and see how well you are learning to obey only my voice without a rope.

Chapter 8

Trusting The Shepherd When There Is Danger

Next it will be helpful to develop principles of discerning danger and learning how to avoid its consequences. The first is to learn from a wise, responsible, or spiritually mature person like a parent or pastor. This person has reliable knowledge of danger and its effects and realizes that we have not yet learned that skill. Thus, they do us a great favor by explaining and alerting us to the features and effects of dangers.

Another way of discerning dangers is from our own personal skills based on our current knowledge and experience of events that are dangerous. The older and more mature we are in our spiritual walk, the more adapt we become in spotting and analyzing dangers on our own.

This discernment often comes from the experience of falling into dangers without understanding beforehand that they were dangerous. Sometimes the effects are small and inconsequential, others may leave us impacted for life. Most of them fall into the classification of "School of Hard Knocks."

We can avoid dangers by avoiding the presence of evil in all its forms and places, and by resisting dangerous practices. We must remember that the dangers exist, and that we need to strengthen our resistance.

Finally, it is helpful to have wise people available to help us resist dangerous practices. Wise sheep-people are aware that there are dangers that are beyond their ability to resist. Consequently, it is commendable wisdom to know to whom and where to go when dangers are beyond our strength.

Now let's turn to the sheep talk that I had with my lamb Cevesh.

"Cevesh, the other morning on the way to the grazing place as we just emerged from the men's dorm, three large dogs were going down the lane. You froze in your tracks and wouldn't move for a long time. Were you afraid of those dogs? I told you it was alright, that I would protect you. Finally, you were willing to follow me again. Then as we went down the lane, two of the large dogs circled around in the field and were headed back toward us. You stopped again and watched them very intently.

"When I saw your fear again, I called you very loudly, more for the dogs' sakes than for yours. When the dogs heard my loud voice, it startled them. They turned and ran very fast, like I had shot at them with a gun. Cevesh, you watched them run so hard and disappear into the bushes at the end of the field. I almost laughed at them and at you. You watched and watched after they were completely gone. Did you think they would return? Finally, you relaxed, and we went to the grazing place."

"Shepherd, the other day when I was following you, all of a sudden I stopped because I heard a very unusual sound. I was trying to figure out where it was coming from. But I had stopped right in a trail of large black ants. I didn't notice it, but they began to crawl up my hind leg while I was standing very still. Suddenly they begin to bite and sting me. I jumped and kicked and tried to get them off. I quickly moved and soon they were all off. But for a few moments I was in real pain until we left their area. I think I should watch more carefully where I stop don't you, Shepherd?"

"Cevesh, you are a smart sheep. When you walk by yourself you never walk in a straight line. You weave from side to side so you can look back over your shoulder to see if any enemy is coming up behind you. That is smart.

"You have unusually good eyesight. When you are grown, you will be able to see between 1,200 meters and 1,500 meters away. Because God created you with protruding eyeballs, you have a wrap-around vision that helps you see predators that are approaching from the side.

"You also have a keen sense of smell and will learn to know the different smells of various predators. When you are grown, all these senses that you have as a lamb will be fully developed.

My student Kia commented, "Cevesh has three enemies: distraction, sheep nature, and old habits. I also have distractions in my life which always drive me away from God, my old sinful nature which always [pulls] me down, and my old sinful habits that always haunt me.

"I'm indebted to Cevesh and especially to his shepherd teaching me such practical lessons. It is my earnest prayer that I will practice all that I learned through them."

Chapter 9

Trusting the Shepherd with the Discipline of Routine

The discipline of routine is created by persistence. It is the day after day practice of doing the same events, at the same time, in the same way. Our bodies and minds have been created to assign certain aspects of their functions as routine. For instance, the intake and elimination of food and drink function best in a pattern of routine, roughly, the same times of practice daily. Though food and drink can keep the body normal and healthy even when not functioning on a regular routine, routine avoids a lot of stress on the body.

Another fruit of routine is that it produces "stresslessness." If one wakes daily with a hodgepodge of possible activities for the day, the tension that it builds can be nerve wracking and creates its own routine, a routine that is not desirable. While routine does not take all the stress out of life, when it is particularly targeted at the repetitive activities that are daily required of us for normal living, it can become an easy and relaxing way of living life.

Another valuable aspect of routine is structure. Structure in our lives can free our minds to plan and use other skills that we possess. Structure allows us the space to produce valuable and meaningful activities. Now we may step by step move through our day without wondering what to do next.

My concluding observation on routine is that it produces a model, even an envious model, of how to live life. People with whom we mingle regularly, especially family members, are quick to observe that our lives are not being lived out in a hodgepodge of activities and frustrations of what to do next. When they see our lives that are "together," they are attracted to them and often become envious of our structured living styles.

"Cevesh, I'd like to talk to you about three things today that have to do with routine. The *joy* of routine with you. It really is a joy to spend consistent time with you each day and watch our relationship develop and grow. We do things together that we could not do one month ago. You have learned fast and are growing.

"The *necessity* of routine. We must stay disciplined if our relationship is going to grow. We must meet every morning that we can. We must do some of the same things every day for you to learn and develop. Routine is necessary for our relationship to deepen and mature and last.

"The *boredom* of routine. For me there are times when I have other things that I need to do. But I have made a commitment to you, so I will spend time with you and for you. A lot depends on my regular schedule. But I admit my committed routine to you can be boring sometimes. Keeping my eye on the goal of your development drives the boredom away."

"Shepherd, I can almost figure out what you are trying to do now. When I see you coming, I know we will be going to the stairs and the classroom. I know that we will go up and down the stairs several times. That I will lie down. That you will brush me and talk to me.

That you will write in your journal. That you will do your exercises on the stairs. Then we will return to the cafeteria."

"Just because I know what we will do does not mean that I am ready or even want to do them. Shepherd, I am learning that knowing and desiring or wanting are totally different matters. Knowledge and will are drastically different. I am still young, but I am learning."

Students perceived the necessity of routine and gave their comments. "A systematic way of training and learning is needed in order that one would attain maturity. The shepherd trained Cevesh regularly and systematically and because of this Cevesh could assimilate in the new culture and slowly and gradually get transformed through the will of his shepherd.

"I feel the greatest need of training and discipline in my life in order that I will reap a healthy Christian life. There is no overnight success. It demands time and perseverance."

Chapter 10

Trusting the Shepherd with Change

Cevesh expressed a resistance to change. "I don't always like all of your decisions. I like to make some of my own decisions, particularly when I don't understand what your decisions are all about. You don't want me to be your slave, do you? Can't I think for myself? God gave me a brain. Don't you think I should use it? If I just follow you all the time, I'll turn it to a robot that never uses his brains for anything creative or constructive."

In the course of our regular activities, we experience changes that we have no control over and probably would never have chosen for ourselves. I call these unsolicited changes. As God's sheep, we realize the sovereignty of God in every detail of our existence. Thus, we are quick to accuse God for "messing up our lives" without soliciting our input or even informing us of the coming changes. These "tornados" of God's sovereignty can plunge us into discouragement and resistance to what God wants to accomplish in our lives according to his before-we-were-born plan.

When we resist God's plans for our lives it makes it difficult for him to work with us in harmony. Having said that, he can still do it. Our resistance does not change his ability to accomplish his will in our lives. But from the middle of the tornado, the unsolicited change appears to be more difficult and often leaves us wandering, "Why God?" That question may never be fully answered. Just maybe he wants us to be able to perceive and accept his wise plans for our lives without our feeling he must discuss with us what has been in his heart for eternity for us. Furthermore, when we do come to this position of acceptance of his will for our lives on our own, God must delight in our relationship of our trust in him far beyond our ability to perceive or express it.

There is a twofold impact that comes from our acceptance of God's unsolicited changes in our lives. Our surrender becomes a teaching model of what other believers in our fellowship should do when God brings unsolicited changes into their lives. Mature believers always stand out in the congregation of sheep. Growing believers wisely observe what's happening in the lives of mature believers and how they handle it. We are all of one body.

We can also impact the unbelieving community of which we are a continuing part. Unbelievers often see the unsolicited changes that "tornados" bring into our lives. The godly maturity with which we handle these often very difficult circumstances can burn deeply into the minds and hearts of our unconverted friends and acquaintances. They may or may not express their observations in words, but the impact is made, nonetheless. When an unbeliever asks for an explanation of how the mature Christian can handle these unsolicited storms of change, he has in essence, opened the door for an opportunity to share the gospel and to invite the unbelieving observer into the sheepfold.

"Shepherd, when you change where I feed, I forget about where you are taking me. I sometimes think that what I have right now is better than what I will have in the future. The here and now is very powerful in my mind. But you have a way of persisting until I leave the present food and go where you have chosen. I always have more variety with you. So, it really is better for you to choose where I'll graze."

Give ear to my student Kia. "I totally understand what Cevesh had gone through. I also have so many things in my life [that] always rob me from my relationship with God. Every little thing I do in life should have eternal values that glorify God. Most the time I am at the other extreme, fulfilling my own desire[s] and love[s]."

Chapter 11

Trusting the Shepherd by Walking Close

This warm topic of a close walk with the shepherd should be the desire of all of God's sheep-people. Certainly, walking closely with someone we love is a desirable and enjoyable experience. In the spiritual realm it exceeds the physical qualities and characteristics of having a close walk with a friend or family member.

Note the two aspects of the term: close and walk. The metaphor is rich and suggests focused action. Close is a relationally defining term. It suggests awareness of presence and potential for interaction. Closeness also suggests attentively watching the actions of the person who is nearby. This involves a decision to stay close relationally and to exert the effort necessary to remain close. These are positive actions that continue a close relationship.

Now let's think about what it means to walk closely with someone. To continue walking closely to someone, we realize that we must stay in sync with the changing location of the one to whom we desire to remain close. Walking also suggests progress, that is leaving one area behind and moving on to a new area, and usually includes a goal to reach in the mind of the one who has planned the walk. Finally, in walking and changing our locations it is necessary to be aware of our surroundings in order to stay upright and functional.

These insights gain clarity as we listen to interchanges between Cevesh and his shepherd.

"Shepherd, I've really enjoyed our mornings together. You know where the good pastures are. You led me, stayed with me, and returned me to my keeper. It was good to be near you and with you. I wasn't afraid when you were close by."

"Cevesh, you totally surprised me the morning of your one-month anniversary. I took your rope off about 50 meters from where you graze by me. I expected you to follow me the rest of the way, but you didn't. You began immediately to graze and would not come when I called. I was a little disappointed. But since you weren't trying to get away, I decided to let you graze where you stopped. After all you had grazed in that same spot a couple of weeks ago, and you knew where the good plants were. But then you really surprised me. After about 5-7 minutes of grazing, you stopped without my calling anymore. You came the whole distance to me without stopping along the way. You came to me and stood for over 35 minutes while I combed, petted, and talked gently to you. We really do have a bond that is developing between you and me.

"Cevesh, I enjoy being with you every morning. I have watched you grow for two and a half months. I watched you learn to follow me. You have learned my voice. You have learned to climb stairs with me. You have learned to lie down and get up. I feel you push gently against my leg. Sometimes you just stand and look at me. All these things I enjoy.

"I have noted that it is better for you to walk *right beside me* rather than *behind me.* When you walk close to me, you are less likely to be distracted by other things, like sounds, people, other animals and even tasty bites of different plants. When you lag behind me you tend to become easily distracted. Sometimes I must persistently call you to come follow me. Other times I even must go back to you to get you to follow me closely again. Yes, *beside is better than behind.*"

"Shepherd, did you notice that the other day I walked right along beside you once we reached the lane to the grazing area? You didn't tug on my rope. I just walked beside you and sometimes I rubbed up against your leg as you were walking. That felt good to me just to be alongside walking in step with you."

"Cevesh, you did something the other day that you hadn't done before. When we were returning to the shed after your morning grazing, you were making sweet little lamb sounds as we were walking. I could barely hear them. They seem to tell me of your complete contentment to be walking with me. They were not loud. They were not demanding. They were not rebellious or even whining. They were just sweet little lamb sounds of contentment, and I heard them very clearly.

"Something very important is happening between us every day. Our relationship is getting stronger and stronger, deeper and deeper. You like to lean against my leg, and we experience a bond getting stronger steadily day after day. But Cevesh this could *never* happen if we had not spent time together every day (except two) for the last 39 days. The formula is simple: concentrated, regular time together creates a rich, growing relationship. Let's keep this good thing going."

"Shepherd, have you noticed lately that I'm not always at the end of my rope while I'm grazing? It feels good to enjoy what is close to you and not always be trying to get what is out of reach. I'm learning that there is plenty of good pasture close to you. Did you plan it that way?

"I noticed that you dropped the rope while I was grazing the other day. At first, I didn't notice it. But after a while I was able to go a little further than I normally do away from you. You did not try to stop me. But that was OK. I really did not want to leave you, so I soon turned back and grazed close to you.

"Did you notice that recently I have been walking almost all the way to and from the grazing place? I have been walking very steadily with you. I know where we are headed and most of the time, I am learning to wait till we get to the good place to graze because I know what is waiting for me."

"Cevesh, I want to talk to you about your voluntary time with me. I have been noticing a pattern developing that I like very much. On several occasions, you will stop grazing and come over to me without me calling you. You just stand there and wait for me to pet or comb you. Sometimes you only stay 1-2 minutes. Other times you will stand by me with your head leaning against my leg for 10-11 minutes. I like that because I didn't call you. You just come on your own voluntary will. You want to be with me. I enjoy that very much, Cevesh.

"There is another matter that is on my heart this morning. Remember the other morning when you started to come over to me and then turned aside and left me. That hurt. I thought you were inclined to spend some time with me like you did a few days ago. I don't want to be oversensitive, but if we are going to be close friends and develop a strong, deep relationship it will take time together, just the two of us focused on each other. How about it, Little Sheep? Let's work on that together, OK?"

"Shepherd, sometimes you get so busy writing in your book I think you may forget me for a moment. The other day while you were writing about me, I walked around behind you and just waited for you to notice me. When you turned around, you were so glad to see me there that you stopped writing and just spent time with me petting and combing my wool and talking to me."

"Cevesh, you have reached a very important day in our relationship. The other day I discarded the rope. You follow me now just by my voice and when I call you. Occasionally, I must take you back by your collar and redirect you momentarily, but you quickly repent and change your ways and follow me. This is an awesome milestone in our relationship. Five weeks ago, you could not have responded to me the way you do today. You hear me, you follow me, and you obey me… not perfectly but very consistently. Now there is no limit in what we can do and learn together. You are on your way to becoming a miracle sheep.

"The last two things I want to mention to you today is about starting out with me and following me to the classroom. Today was the first time that when I came to get you that you turned around and left me and did not want to go with me. What is going on here? However, once we got started you followed so well. You left the yellow blossoms alone. You walked closely to me. I don't think you even stopped once on our whole trip out. Now how can you be so good on the trip but not want to get started? You have me guessing about what is going on in your little lamb brain.

Students have absorbed many insights and lesson. Let's begin with Sudeep's reflections.

"It is a wonderful experience to learn from Cevesh. It is like getting the practical example for building a new church or discipling a new believer. There are so many things that I could say, but the most important is to be patient in ministry because things will not happen the way we think. We need to know people's needs and desires to teach them. Also, how to handle a new believer, we need to teach and disciple them continuously, so that they can be well-trained and have good knowledge. Another thing is building the relationship with one another, spending time together, these things are important in the ministry."

Next listen to Kia's lessons. "There're two lessons I've learned from Cevesh. 1. Reluctance to follow and obey the Shepherd because he is in a new relationship. Sheep do not try to obey his Master but due to his old nature he most of the time was carried away by the desires of his own. Only to this nature he failed the experience and the blessing which his master desires for him. The shepherd also needs to understand the sheep because everything is new to the sheep. Patience with compassion and love and care are the elements a shepherd needs to have in his relationship with his sheep. 2. The shepherd needs to have a strong connection with God, who is the ultimate owner of the sheep. You must realize that he is the under shepherd from God for the sheep. He must love God in order that he may love the sheep as God loves his sheep."

I'll close this chapter with Binal's comments. "I'm inspired by Cevesh because he desires to follow the shepherd. At the beginning he was lazy and did not follow the shepherd. Always the shepherd had the rope on his neck and bring him to class. But after a few days he came to recognize his master. Whenever he heard the master's sound he will look here and there and follow. Now the shepherd does not need a rope around his neck. He can follow easily after his master, whenever he listens carefully for the master's voice."

Chapter 12

Trusting the Shepherd with the Future

Animals have a measure of ability to anticipate the future. Bears hibernate, and squirrels gather nuts. Many animals anticipate the winter and grow a heavier coat of fur, then shed their winter coats in anticipations of warm weather. Anticipating the future is common ground for animals and man, though on considerably different levels of awareness.

The relationship between the Good Shepherd and us has a continuing future. No end is announced or defined in the relationship. Consequently, one naturally begins to anticipate what the future will hold in the relationship. In my relationship with Cevesh, he anticipated the future when I came to his pen in the mornings and was already waiting for me.

Anticipating the future is reflected in one's daily routine when there is preparation for the "next step" of the future day's activity. This is true for things in the near future as well as in the distant future.

Consistent correction can lead you to change your behavior in the future. For example, when I led Cevesh out to graze, we came to a "Y" in the trail or a cross path where I had *corrected* him several times in the past. Anticipating that I would *correct* him again, he turned to the correct lane of his own volition.

In anticipating the future, no one knows the details. For the believer, though he has informational promises in the Word of God which anticipates the future, there are major areas of detail that are missing. When details are missing, we still need to trust the shepherd. God intends for us to totally trust him who has the complete plan in mind and knows all the details of our anticipated future.

The Bible is replete with structured future events with enough detail in the text that the events can be recognized and anticipated with full trustworthiness of the Shepherd. Likewise, Cevesh, though void of any

Bible knowledge, knows each morning what to anticipate throughout the future of the day.

Cevesh showed me how he anticipated the future end of his grazing time. "Cevesh, the other day as we returned to your shed, when I took your rope off you followed me all the way back until we almost reached the shed. Then you surprised me again. You broke out in a fast run passing me up and going the rest of the way by yourself. Yes, you really do have a good anticipating memory."

CONCLUSION

I have covered a lot of ground in unfolding the experiences I had with training my young lamb Cevesh and taking him into the classroom of the young pastors in my course of pastoral ministry.

My primary goal in my classroom in India was preparing students for pastoral ministry. However, along the way, I dropped comments appropriate for veteran experienced pastors. I wanted to spotlight new believers in the congregation that needed gentle care, and I suggested pastoral principles in getting older sheep, mature believers, to follow their shepherd.

My primary goal through this book has been taking the lessons I learned in my care of Cevesh and applying them to learning to trust the shepherd on our spiritual journey.

My student Kia explains the relationship of the metaphor between my lamb Cevesh and me, the shepherd, best.

"Cevesh enjoyed his life with his original family, he never thought that there would be life beyond what he had with his family. But a day came when he had to leave his loved ones and belong to someone else. He had no clues of what his tomorrow would be. The new shepherd bought him with a price from his old master so that he would train and equip him for a greater purpose. He was the chosen one among the flock of sheep, chosen not by his strength or ability but by the sheer mercy of the shepherd who purchased him. The lamb had no contribution in the transaction; it was all done by the shepherd.

"It reminds me of the day I experienced the saving grace of God. Better than ever, I was able to see a picture vividly through the life of Cevesh. The day I got saved was the happiest day of my life. I never pictured my experience as simple and clear as what I got through Cevesh."

Thank you, students.

Indeed, if you have learned to trust Jesus as the Good Shepherd and seen yourself as a sheep in this spiritual metaphorical journey, I have accomplished my purpose. God bless you!

Thank you, Reader, for joining us on this journey.

Could you help us spread the news about *Trust the Shepherd?*

A review on Amazon or a mention on social media to your circle helps immensely. Thank you!

Made in the USA
Monee, IL
21 December 2022